Provided
by

Measure B

which was approved by
the voters in
November, 1998

EXPLORING DINOSAURS & PREHISTORIC CREATURES

SABER-TOOTHED CATS

By Susan H. Gray

THE CHILD'S WORLD®
CHANHASSEN, MINNESOTA

Published in the United States of America by The Child's World®
PO Box 326, Chanhassen, MN 55317-0326
800-599-READ
www.childsworld.com

Content Adviser:
Brian Huber, PhD,
Curator, Department
of Paleobiology,
Smithsonian
National Museum
of Natural History,
Washington DC

Photo Credits: Soqui Ted/Corbis Sygma: 15; Tom Brakefield/Corbis: 19; Craig Aurness/Corbis: 23; Douglas Henderson: 20; Michael Long/The Natural History Museum, London: 6, 11, 22, 26; The Natural History Museum, London: 7, 17; Peter Snowball/The Natural History Museum, London: 14; Tom McHugh/Natural History Museum of L.A. County/Photo Researchers, Inc.: 5; Sinclair Stammers/Photo Researchers, Inc.: 8, 24; Joe Tucciarone/Photo Researchers, Inc.: 10; Tom McHugh/California Academy of Sciences/Photo Researchers, Inc.: 12, 21; Nigel J. Dennis/Photo Researchers, Inc.: 16; Victor Habbick Visions/Photo Researchers, Inc.: 25; Tom McHugh/Photo Researchers, Inc.: 27; Tom & Therisa Stack/Tom Stack & Assoc.: 13.

The Child's World®: Mary Berendes, Publishing Director

Editorial Directions, Inc.: E. Russell Primm, Editorial Director; Pam Rosenberg, Line Editor; Katie Marsico, Associate Editor; Matthew Messbarger, Editorial Assistant; Susan Hindman, Copy Editor; Melissa McDaniel, Proofreader; Tim Griffin/IndexServ, Indexer; Olivia Nellums, Fact Checker; Dawn Friedman, Photo Researcher; Linda S. Koutris, Photo Selector

Original cover art by Todd Marshall

The Design Lab: Kathleen Petelinsek, Design; Kari Thornborough, Page Production

Library of Congress Cataloging-in-Publication Data
Gray, Susan Heinrichs
  Saber-toothed cats / by Susan H. Gray.
    p. cm. — (Exploring dinosaurs & prehistoric creatures)
  Includes index.
  ISBN 1-59296-412-5 (lib. bd. : alk. paper) 1. Saber-toothed tigers—Juvenile literature. I. Title.
  QE882.C15G78 2005
  569'.75—dc22   2004018082

TABLE OF CONTENTS

CHAPTER ONE

NOT SO LUCKY

I t looked like the start of a great evening for *Smilodon* (SMY-loh-don). The weather was perfect, and the saber-toothed (SAY-bur-tootht) cat had just finished a long nap. He stretched his legs and yawned a big, slow yawn. Then he sat quietly for a minute, squinting at the setting sun. That's when he heard it—the cry of a wolf in the distance.

The cat's ears twitched. He turned his head toward the sound and peered across the land. He saw nothing, but he heard the cries grow louder. *Smilodon* rose up and began to trot toward the noise. He was a heavyset, muscular cat, not a fast runner. He kept up his pace for a minute and then stopped in his tracks. He saw the wolf, and he saw why it was howling. The wolf was thrashing and twisting about, but its

*Saber-toothed cats were predators. This means they hunted
other animals, such as this dire wolf, for food.*

feet were not moving. They were stuck to something, and the wolf

could not pull them free. What a lucky find for *Smilodon*! He could

start his night with an easy kill.

Smilodon trotted closer to the wolf and pounced, sinking his teeth

into the wolf's belly. This was almost too easy. Then something went

terribly wrong. The saber-toothed cat tried to pull away from the wolf,

Smilodon *attack a mammoth that is trapped in a tar pit.*

but he couldn't. His hind legs were knee-deep in sticky, black tar, and

his paws were glued to the wolf's body by the gooey muck. The two

animals were locked together, twisting and squirming. As they strug-

gled, they began to sink. Soon they were neck-deep in the sticky gunk.

The sun slowly disappeared, and stars began to twinkle overhead.

By nightfall, there was no sign left of *Smilodon* or his lucky find.

CHAPTER TWO

WHAT WERE SABER-TOOTHED CATS?

Saber-toothed cats were **mammals** that lived from tens of millions of years ago to 10,000 years ago. The cats were carnivores (KAR-nih-vores), or meat-eating animals. They lived in North America, South America, Europe, Africa, and Asia.

The sabertooths are named for the two large teeth shaped like swords, or sabers, that are found in their upper jaws. These big teeth,

Saber-toothed cats, such as these Smilodon, *lived millions of years ago.*

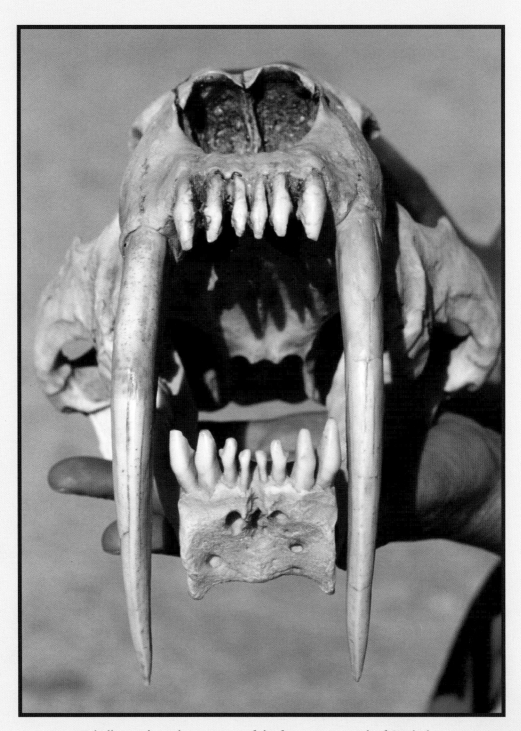

A skull provides a close-up view of the fierce canine teeth of Smilodon.

with roots going far up into the skull, were their canine

(KAY-nine) teeth. Meat-eating animals have canines in both

their upper and lower rows of teeth. Human beings have canines

that are the same length as the rest of their teeth. Saber-toothed

cats, like many hunting animals, had canines that were longer

than their other teeth. These long canines were very good at

piercing flesh.

Like other types of cats, sabertooths were fur-covered animals

that hunted **prey.** They did not eat plant material because they

could not digest it properly. Sabertooths had muscular bodies and

heavy skulls. They had short tails, much like modern-day bobcats.

No one knows exactly what color these animals were. However,

many scientists believe they had tan coats that helped them blend

in with the tall grasses in their **environment.**

Saber-toothed cats are sometimes called saber-toothed tigers, but they were not tigers. Sabertooths have heavier, more muscular bodies than tigers and much shorter tails.

Although some people call these cats saber-toothed tigers, this

is not really a correct name. Tigers are slender, striped animals

with long tails. Tigers and saber-toothed cats are different

members of the cat family. Panthers, lions, jaguars, and house

cats are some other members of the family.

CHAPTER THREE

DAGGERS AND BLADES

There were two different kinds of saber-toothed cats. Some, called dirk-toothed cats, had extremely long teeth. *Dirk* is a Scottish word for "dagger." The dirk-toothed cats were stocky animals, with muscular legs and bodies. Their canine teeth were up to 7 inches (18 centimeters) long. The cats opened their mouths wide to chomp down on prey animals. They also had especially strong neck muscles that made it possible for them to deliver fatal wounds.

The other type of sabertooth is called the

*Megantereon (MEG-an-TEHR-ee-awn) was a dirk-toothed cat. Some scientists believe Megantereon sometimes preyed on **ancient** humans.*

scimitar-toothed (SIM-ih-tar-tootht) cat. A scimitar is a sword with

a broad, curved blade. Scimitar-toothed cats had shorter, broader

canines than their dirk-toothed cousins. Their canine teeth were only

about 4 inches (10 cm) long, but they still could deliver fatal wounds.

These cats had longer limbs and were probably better runners than

the dirktooths.

Homotherium *(HO-mo-THER-ee-um), a scimitar-toothed cat, prepares to eat an impala.*

Some bones discovered in 1983 show that there might have been a third kind of sabertooth. The skeletons are from ancient cats that had teeth more like the scimitar cats, but short, stocky bodies more like the dirktooths.

A Dinictis *(dy-NICK-tis) skull on display.* Dinictis *had teeth similar to those of saber-toothed cats, but scientists disagree on whether or not it was a true sabertooth.*

All saber-toothed cats had special teeth behind their canines. These teeth are called carnassials (kar-NASS-ee-uhlz). As the cat chewed its meat, the carnassials acted like big scissors, cutting and shredding the food to pieces.

LIFE WAS THE PITS

Thousands of years ago, wild animals roamed the area that is now Los Angeles, California. Mastodons and shaggy mammoths lumbered across the land, yanking up plants and eating them. Horses and bison roamed freely. Dire wolves—extinct animals that had heavy skulls and small brains—trotted about, preying on smaller animals. And saber-toothed cats kept watchful eyes on them all.

Food and water were plentiful throughout the area. There were streams and watering holes. There were terrific places for napping in the sun, and cool spots for relaxing in the shade. And there were dangerous places where sticky, black tar oozed from the ground.

The tar came from deep inside the Earth. As it bubbled up, it spread out into black, shiny pools. Animals not paying attention ran,

hopped, or flew into the pools by accident. Some of the stronger animals were able to pull free, but weaker ones became hopelessly trapped.

Thousands of years later, people in Los Angeles discovered the animal graveyards and named them the La Brea (luh BRAY-uh) Tar Pits. In the early 1900s, scientists began pulling fossils from the tar pits and cleaning them up. Since then, they have found more than 3 million fossils. Some of these were the bones of mammoths, mastodons, camels, bears, and ground sloths. The most common large mammal found in the pits is the dire wolf.

In second place is the saber-toothed cat. More than 2,000 sabertooths have been found there.

The ground at La Brea still oozes today. But now the area is protected, and the pit's only victims are moths, flies, and other very small creatures. Scientists are still taking fossils out of the muck, and every year they find more remains of ancient life.

CHAPTER FOUR

HOW DID SABER-TOOTHED CATS SPEND THEIR TIME?

Although scientists have no living saber-toothed cats to study,

they can tell us plenty about the cats' everyday activities.

Paleontologists (PAY-lee-un-TAWL-uh-jists) and zoologists (zoe-AWL-

uh-jists) know a lot about these cats. Paleontologists are people who

Scientists put a collar with a tracking device on a tranquilized leopard.
Zoologists study living animals, and what they learn can help
paleontologists figure out how ancient animals might have behaved.

study ancient plants and animals by looking at their fossil remains. Zoologists are people who study living animals.

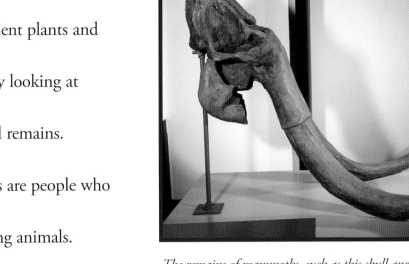

The remains of mammoths, such as this skull and tusks, are often found near places where saber-toothed cats lived and hunted.

Paleontologists have learned a lot from saber-toothed cat skeletons that were found in a Texas cave. In that same cave, they discovered hundreds of teeth from young mammoths. The scientists believe that more than 30 cats lived together in the cave. They probably hunted, ate, and slept together as a group. Scientists believe that the adult cats killed small mammoths and then dragged their bodies to the cave where the whole group could feed.

Paleontologists have also found sabertooth bones showing that the cats often became sick or wounded. This is proof that life was not always easy even for the mighty sabertooths. Some bones show signs of healing. This may mean that groups of cats protected their sickly members until they recovered.

Zoologists who study modern-day cats believe that saber-tooths probably had two different hunting methods. The heavy, muscular, dirk-toothed cats were not fast runners. They did not have the slender bodies, long legs, and long tails necessary for speed and balance. They probably hid and waited for their prey to come along. Then they leaped out and attacked with one powerful bite. The scimitar-toothed cats had a lighter build and longer legs. These cats probably chased down their prey.

Zoologists also believe that saber-toothed cats could roar. They know this by looking at certain bones from the throat. The throat

An African lion roars. Scientists believe that saber-toothed cats could roar because their throat bones are similar to those of lions and other roaring cats.

bones of sabertooths match those of roaring cats such as tigers, lions, and leopards. The bones are different from those of mountain lions and house cats, which cannot roar.

CHAPTER FIVE

A Look at Some Saber-Toothed Cats

Scientists have discovered several different kinds of saber-toothed cats. The most common one is *Smilodon*, whose name means "knife tooth" in Greek. It is the one most people picture when they think of saber-toothed cats. *Smilodon* was common around the La Brea Tar Pits, but it also roamed through-out North America, South America, and Europe. It was about

Saber-toothed cats roamed almost everywhere on Earth. Their remains have been found in North America, South America, Europe, Africa, and Asia.

A Megantereon rests with its young cub.

5 feet (1.5 meters) long and about 3 feet (1 m) tall at the shoulder.

The animal weighed about 440 pounds (200 kilograms). A dirk-

toothed cat, it hunted by springing on its prey in surprise attacks.

Smilodon probably hunted mastodons, horses, deer, buffalo,

and wolves. It might also have eaten animals that had already died.

Megantereon lived in Africa, Asia, Europe, and North America.

Like *Smilodon,* it had huge saber teeth in its upper jaw. Its chinbone

A pack of Homotherium *feed on their prey.*

flared out in such a way as to protect those teeth when the mouth

was closed.

   Homotherium was a scimitar-toothed cat that was about the size of

a lion. Its front legs were longer than its back legs, and it was probably

a good runner and jumper. *Homotherium* is the cat that lived in the

Texas cave and ate baby mammoths.

THE TOOTH PROBLEM

How exactly did saber-toothed cats use their big teeth to kill? Could the cats just jump on prey animals and sink their teeth in them? Did they use their teeth to stab or to rip? Could the teeth snap bones? Did those enormous teeth ever get in their way? These are questions that have puzzled scientists for years.

Scientists believe that sabertooths must have had a very special killing method. If a cat jumped onto the back of a prey animal and bit into the neck, its teeth would have hit neck bones. But the canine teeth of saber-toothed cats were brittle and easily broken. If they hit bone, they would shatter.

If a dirk-toothed cat sank its teeth into a large prey animal and held on, the prey would struggle fiercely to escape. In fact, it could probably struggle hard enough to break off the cat's teeth or even pull them out by the roots.

Scientists think that perhaps the saber-toothed cats sank their teeth into the soft areas of their prey. By biting into muscle, throat, or belly tissue, the cats would not have hit bone. Then maybe they pulled away from their prey and waited for it to die. The scimitar-toothed cats may have held on to their struggling prey, because their teeth were too short to be yanked out.

Some scientists believe that the canine teeth were not used for hunting at all. They may instead have been for attracting mates. Without any living saber-toothed cats to study, we might never know exactly how these cats used their teeth.

CHAPTER SIX

THE END OF AN AGE

Saber-toothed cats lived during a time when Earth was going

through an ice age. This may sound like the whole planet was

freezing cold, but that was not the case. Temperatures all over the world

were several degrees cooler than they are today. In some places, this was

enough to make water freeze into **glaciers.** In other areas, it was

*Some saber-toothed cats were well-equipped to handle the icy conditions
that existed in many places on Earth during the most recent ice age.*

Mastodons looked a lot like modern-day elephants, but there are many differences between the two animals. Mastodons were not as tall as elephants, and their ears were smaller. In addition, the ancient mastodons were covered with long hair.

enough to make the air cool, but not freezing.

Earth has actually gone through several ice ages in its history. The most recent one started about 1.6 million years ago and ended about 10,000 years ago. During this ice age, much of North America, Europe, and Asia were covered in great ice sheets. Parts of Africa, Australia, and South America were covered as well.

Despite the cold temperatures, many great land animals thrived. In North America, these were mastodons, mammoths, giant ground sloths, and saber-toothed cats. Horses, wolves, wild pigs, and camels also roamed the land. For some reason, many of these animals—including the saber-toothed cats—vanished at the end of the ice age.

Scientists are not sure what caused the sabertooths to die out. Some say that humans killed them all by hunting. Some believe that diseases wiped out the animals. Others think that the cats simply could not get used to the warmer temperatures as the ice age ended. Maybe all these things worked against the sabertooths. Whatever the reason, the mighty saber-toothed cats disappeared forever, leaving only their fossils behind.

A Smilodon skeleton on display. Today the only way to see a saber-toothed cat is in a museum exhibit.

Glossary

ancient (AYN-shunt) Something that is ancient is very old; from thousands or even millions of years ago. Paleontologists study ancient life.

environment (en-VYE-ruhn-muhnt) An environment is made up of the things that surround a living creature, such as the air and soil. Many scientists believe that saber-toothed cats had tan coats that helped them blend in with the tall grasses in their environment.

extinct (ek-STINGKT) Something that is extinct has died out and no longer exists. Dire wolves are extinct animals that had heavy skulls and small brains.

fossils (FOSS-uhlz) Fossils are the things left behind by ancient plants or animals, such as skeletons or footprints. Scientists have found many saber-toothed cat fossils in the La Brea Tar Pits.

glaciers (GLAY-shurz) Glaciers are huge ice formations. During an ice age, snow accumulates more than it melts, causing much of the Earth to be covered by glaciers.

ground sloths (GROUND SLAWTHS) Ground sloths are extinct mammals that are related to South American tree-dwelling sloths. Ground sloth fossils have been found at the La Brea Tar Pits.

mammals (MAM-uhlz) Mammals are animals that are warm-blooded, have backbones and hair (or fur), and feed their young with milk made by the bodies of the mothers. Saber-toothed cats were mammals that died out about 10,000 years ago.

prey (PRAY) Animals that are hunted and eaten by others are called prey. Sabertooths were fur-covered animals that hunted prey.

Did You Know?

▶ *Smilodon* is the state fossil of California.

▶ Saber-toothed cats are often confused with animals called false saber-toothed cats. The false sabertooths appeared earlier in Earth's history. They had skulls that were different from those of true cats, and they were not members of the cat family.

▶ Some scientists believe that saber-toothed cats in Africa may have hunted early humans.

How to Learn More

AT THE LIBRARY

Hehner, Barbara, and Mark Hallett (illustrator). *Ice Age Sabertooth: The Most Ferocious Cat That Ever Lived.*
New York: Crown Publishers, 2002.

Matthews, Rupert. *Sabertooth.* Chicago: Heinemann Library, 2003.

Palmer, Douglas, Barry Cox (editor). *The Simon & Schuster Encyclopedia of Dinosaurs & Prehistoric Creatures: A Visual Who's Who of Prehistoric Life.* New York: Simon & Schuster, 1999.

ON THE WEB

Visit our home page for lots of links about saber-toothed cats:
http://www.childsworld.com/links.html
NOTE TO PARENTS, TEACHERS, AND LIBRARIANS: We routinely verify our Web links
to make sure they're safe, active sites—so encourage your readers to check them out!

PLACES TO VISIT OR CONTACT

AMERICAN MUSEUM OF NATURAL HISTORY
To view fossils of saber-toothed cats and other ancient mammals
Central Park West at 79th Street
New York, NY 10024-5192
212/769-5100

PAGE MUSEUM AT THE LA BREA TAR PITS
To see the famous tar pits and the fossils that have been found there
5801 Wilshire Boulevard
Los Angeles, CA 90036
323/934-7243

SMITHSONIAN NATIONAL MUSEUM OF NATURAL HISTORY
To see saber-toothed cat fossils and learn more about ice age mammals
10th Street and Constitution Avenue NW
Washington, DC 20560-0166
202/357-2700

The Geologic Time Scale

CAMBRIAN PERIOD

Date: 540 million to 505 million years ago
Most major animal groups appeared by the end of this period. Trilobites were common and algae became more diversified.

ORDOVICIAN PERIOD

Date: 505 million to 440 million years ago
Marine life became more diversified. Crinoids and blastoids appeared, as did corals and primitive fish. The first land plants appeared. The climate changed greatly during this period—it began as warm and moist, but temperatures ultimately dropped. Huge glaciers formed, causing sea levels to fall.

SILURIAN PERIOD

Date: 440 million to 410 million years ago Glaciers melted, sea levels rose, and Earth's climate became more stable. Plants with vascular systems developed. This means they had parts that helped them to conduct food and water.

DEVONIAN PERIOD

Date: 410 million to 360 million years ago
Fish became more diverse, as did land plants. The first trees and forests appeared at this time, and the earliest seed-bearing plants began to grow. The first land-living vertebrates and insects appeared. Fossils also reveal evidence of the first ammonoids and amphibians. The climate was warm and mild.

CARBONIFEROUS PERIOD

Date: 360 million to 286 million years ago
The climate was warm and humid, but cooled toward the end of the period. Coal swamps dotted the landscape, as did a multitude of ferns. The earliest reptiles existed. Pelycosaurs such as *Edaphosaurus* evolved toward the end of the Carboniferous period.

PERMIAN PERIOD

Date: 286 million to 248 million years ago
Algae, sponges, and corals were common on the ocean floor. Amphibians and reptiles were also prevalent at this time, as were seed-bearing plants and conifers. This period ended with the largest mass extinction on Earth. This may have been caused by volcanic activity or the formation of glaciers and the lowering of sea levels.

TRIASSIC PERIOD

Date: 248 million to 208 million years ago
The climate during this period was warm and dry. The first true mammals appeared, as did frogs, salamanders, and lizards. Evergreen trees made up much of the plant life. The first dinosaurs, including *Coelophysis*, existed. In the skies, pterosaurs became the earliest winged reptiles to take flight. In the seas, ichthyosaurs and plesiosaurs made their appearance.

JURASSIC PERIOD

Date: 208 million to 144 million years ago
The climate of the Jurassic period was warm and moist. The first birds appeared at this time, and plant life was more diverse and widespread. Although dinosaurs didn't even exist in the beginning of the Triassic period, they ruled Earth by Jurassic times. *Allosaurus, Apatosaurus, Archaeopteryx, Brachiosaurus, Compsognathus, Diplodocus, Ichthyosaurus, Plesiosaurus,* and *Stegosaurus* were just a few of the prehistoric creatures that lived during this period.

CRETACEOUS PERIOD

Date: 144 million to 65 million years ago
The climate of the Cretaceous period was fairly mild. Many modern plants developed, including those with flowers. With flowering plants came a greater diversity of insect life. Birds further developed into two types: flying and flightless. Prehistoric creatures such as *Ankylosaurus, Edmontosaurus, Iguanodon, Maiasaura, Oviraptor, Psittacosaurus, Spinosaurus, Triceratops, Troodon, Tyrannosaurus rex,* and *Velociraptor* all existed during this period. At the end of the Cretaceous period came a great mass extinction that wiped out the dinosaurs, along with many other groups of animals.

TERTIARY PERIOD

Date: 65 million to 1.8 million years ago
Mammals were extremely diversified at this time, and modern-day creatures such as horses, dogs, cats, bears, and whales developed.

QUATERNARY PERIOD

Date: 1.8 million years ago to today
Temperatures continued to drop during this period. Several periods of glacial development led to what is known as the Ice Age. Prehistoric creatures such as glyptodonts, mammoths, mastodons, *Megatherium,* and saber-toothed cats roamed the land. A mass extinction of these animals occurred approximately 10,000 years ago. The first human beings evolved during the Quaternary period.

Index

About the Author

Susan H. Gray has bachelor's and master's degrees in zoology and has taught college-level courses in biology. She first fell in love with fossil hunting while studying paleontology in college. In her 25 years as an author, she has written many articles for scientists and researchers, and many science books for children. Susan enjoys gardening, traveling, and playing the piano. She and her husband, Michael, live in Cabot, Arkansas.